Luis Palau

W. Terry Whalin

Illustrated by
Ken Landgraf

BARBOUR
PUBLISHING, INC.
Uhrichsville, Ohio

Published by Barbour Publishing, Inc., P.O. Box 719, Uhrichsville, Ohio 44683 http://www.barbourbooks.com

 Member of the
Evangelical Christian
Publishers Association

Printed in the United States of America.

Luis Palau

THAT SON WAS CHRISTENED LUIS PALAU JR.

1

The church bell sounded in the small riverside resort town of Ingeniero-Maschwitz, Argentina, located in the eastern province of Buenos Aires. A crowd gathered in the Catholic church—the only church in town. When the priest called them forward, Luis and Matilde Palau walked to the front. In her arms, Matilde carried their first-born son.

On November 27, 1934, that son was christened Luis Palau Jr. This tiny baby was beginning a life that would bring thousands of people into a personal relationship with Jesus Christ.

Luis Palau Sr. built a thriving construction business. When Luis Jr. was born, his father was a nonreligious person. His mother attended church, searching for real answers to life's questions. Then the Palaus met Edward Rogers.

As an executive with the Shell Oil Company, Mr. Rogers worked in Argentina. He looked for opportunities to win people to Christ. He and his wife developed a friendship with the Palaus and gave them a copy of the gospel of Matthew.

Matilde Palau read the book on her knees. When she reached the Beatitudes, she learned that the pure in heart shall see God. She knew her heart wasn't pure. *This is the kind of life I want to live,* she said to herself. *I won't settle for anything less.* Mr. and Mrs. Rogers led Matilde Palau to Christ, but Mr. Palau didn't want anything to do with what he called "evangelical stuff."

MATILDE PALAU READ THE BOOK ON HER KNEES.

Mrs. Palau began attending the Christian Brethren church where Mr. Rogers sometimes preached. She asked her husband to go with her, but he refused. Every so often, however, he was seen standing outside the corrugated-metal shed where the Christian Brethren worshiped. He was listening to the sermons.

One day Mr. Palau reluctantly agreed to attend church with his wife and walked into the small chapel. The Palaus sat together, holding one-and-a-half-year-old Luisito, as Luis Jr. was called. Mr. Rogers preached that morning. As Mr. Palau listened to the sermon, he thought about what he had heard over the weeks as he stood in the shadows outside the church. The Holy Spirit convicted him.

Mr. Palau realized the time had come for him to make a decision. And he knew what that decision must be. Without waiting for the sermon to end, he stood up. Using a statement often made by evangelicals in Argentina at that time, he said, "I receive

THE TIME HAD COME FOR HIM TO MAKE A DECISION.

Jesus Christ as my only and sufficient Savior."

Matilde Palau nearly fainted. She was thrilled that her husband would now share her faith, but at the same time she was embarrassed by how he had interrupted the sermon. She hadn't expected her husband to make such a scene.

Almost overnight, Mr. Palau became an active Christian. Few evangelical Christians lived in the town, so the Palaus plunged into Bible study and prayer to learn more about their new faith. Mr. Palau became known for the boldness with which he shared Christ with other people.

As the baby Luis grew up, he watched his parents' activities. Many times he saw his father share his faith and his mother read the Bible. Luis was proud that his parents were committed Christians.

Growing up, Luis spent time with his dad whenever possible. Early in the morning, he often heard his dad open the wood stove to start a fire. Luis would open his eyes and watch his father get

HE OFTEN HEARD HIS DAD OPEN THE WOOD STOVE.

the house ready for the day ahead. If he watched long enough, Luis saw his father slip into his office study—a little room along the side of the house. Turning to a chapter in Proverbs, the distinguished man dropped to his knees for prayer and Bible reading.

One day, his father told Luis that each day he read a chapter of Proverbs. There were thirty-one chapters of Proverbs and often thirty-one days in a month. When he grew older, Luis started the same practice—and has continued this pattern he learned from his father throughout his adult life.

Everyone in the Palau family knew about Luis' temper. If something was wrong or Luis didn't get his way, his temper flared. In a soccer game, the Palau boy gained a reputation for using foul language whenever he felt his team received unfair treatment. Other times at home, Luis would suddenly fly off the handle. He wasn't proud of his anger, but didn't know how to handle it.

IN A SOCCER GAME, THE PALAU BOY GAINED A REPUTATION
FOR USING FOUL LANGUAGE.

Early on, Luis attended a government public school. When Luis reached age seven, his father decided to send him to Quilmes Preparatory School. This private British boarding school was located about twenty miles south of Buenos Aires and a little more than forty miles from his home. Lessons were taught in both English and Spanish. World War II, which was destroying Europe and the Pacific, seemed far away.

Luis was one of fifty boarders at the school. Another two hundred boys and girls joined the school for the day classes. Quilmes was excellent preparation for St. Alban's College, which Luis was scheduled to attend when he reached age ten.

Just after his tenth birthday, Luis took his final exams at Quilmes and started to pack for his trip home for the summer (which begins in the middle of December in Argentina). School would be out until the end of summer.

As he worked in his room, Luis got a message

EARLY ON, LUIS ATTENDED A GOVERNMENT PUBLIC SCHOOL.

that he had a phone call. Hurrying to the phone, he picked up the receiver and heard his grandmother's voice.

"Luis," she said, "your dad is very sick. We really have to pray for him." Although Grandma gave no details, Luis had a terrible feeling.

The next morning, December 17, 1944, Grandma arrived at the school to take Luis to the train station. The three-hour train trip seemed to take forever. Luis could barely stand the suspense and couldn't seem to shake the terrible feelings. Finally, the train arrived in Ingeniero-Maschwitz, and the ten-year-old anxiously hurried toward home.

Any shred of hope for his father evaporated as Luis got within earshot of his house. He could hear his aunts and uncles moaning and crying. As Luis ran through the gate, some of his relatives tried to stop him, but he brushed them aside. His father was lying in bed like he was sleeping, but he looked terrible. His skin was yellow and

THE THREE-HOUR TRAIN TRIP SEEMED TO TAKE FOREVER.

bloated, and his lips were cracked.

Ignoring his four sisters and his other relatives, Luis ran to his father's side and threw his arms around him. But his father's spirit was gone. Luis' mother placed her hands on the young boy's shoulders.

"Luisito, Luisito," she said softly, pulling her son away. "I must talk to you and tell you how it was."

Only ten days earlier, Mr. Palau had gotten sick with bronchial pneumonia. Nothing could be done. Although penicillin was often used to treat pneumonia, it was in short supply. Most medical supplies were being used in Europe and the Pacific to help wounded soldiers involved in the war that had been going on for five years.

Luis' mother said, "We decided to call you so you could hurry home. It was obvious that he was dying, and we gathered around his bed, praying and trying to comfort him. He was struggling to breathe, but suddenly he sat up and began to sing."

MR. PALAU HAD GOTTEN SICK WITH BRONCHIAL PNEUMONIA.

Mrs. Palau continued. "Then, when Papito could no longer hold up his head, he fell back on the pillow and said, 'I'm going to be with Jesus, which is far better.'"

Two hours later, at age thirty-five, Luis Palau Sr. had died. His death was in contrast to the typical death scene in the Palaus' town. Often the dying person would cry out in fear of going to hell. Mr. Palau had felt only peace, knowing that he was going to be with Jesus.

As he stood by his father's body, ten-year-old Luis was overwhelmed with grief and anger at everyone and everything. Death was all too real for Luis. One day his father was there, and the next he was gone.

Throughout that summer, Luis peppered his mother with questions about heaven, the second coming of Christ, and the resurrection. Matilde Palau had been a student of the Scriptures for eight years, so she patiently answered her son's questions

LUIS PEPPERED HIS MOTHER WITH QUESTIONS ABOUT HEAVEN.

and dealt with her own grief. Before Luis returned to school, he settled his questions about eternity and heaven. Without any doubt, Luis knew that his father was in heaven with Jesus Christ.

LUIS KNEW THAT HIS FATHER WAS IN HEAVEN WITH JESUS CHRIST.

LUIS PREPARED TO GO TO ST. ALBAN'S COLLEGE.

2

Three months after his father died, Luis prepared to go to St. Alban's College and continue his education. Luis' dreams about education were faced with indifference by many of the people around him, but his mother was determined to follow her husband's wishes.

During the summer break, Mrs. Palau hired someone to manage the family business. She had never been involved in the day-to-day operation of the company. Money had never been a problem in the Palau family, and Luis left for school with the assumption that the family money would never end.

St. Alban's was a tough, all-boys Anglican school. The Argentine government required Spanish education for at least four hours a day, five days a week. Because St. Alban's was a British school, the teachers taught the morning in Spanish and then the rest of the day in English. Different lessons were taught in Spanish than in English. In this bilingual environment, Luis received two years of schooling during each year. When a student completed the four years at St. Alban's, he was prepared for graduate work at Cambridge University. Luis earned pretty good grades, and his days at the school were happy and filled with pranks and practical jokes.

The only dark spot in Luis' life was the news that the manager his mother had hired was not running the business well. For the first time in Luis'

THE TEACHERS TAUGHT THE MORNING IN SPANISH
AND THE REST OF THE DAY IN ENGLISH.

life, his family was facing a tight financial situation.

During the days before Luis' summer vacation at the end of 1946, Charles Cohen, a St. Alban's professor, talked with Luis about attending a two-week Christian camp in the mountains along with several dozen other boys. While Luis thought it sounded like fun, he didn't want to give up part of his summer vacation.

Because of his Christian upbringing, Luis could quote Bible verses and sing Christian songs. If pressured, he could even say a prayer. But in his heart, Luis knew he wasn't a Christian.

When Luis discussed going to camp with Mr. Cohen, he protested, saying his family finances were too tight. Then Mr. Cohen offered to pay for the camp. So twelve-year-old Luis agreed. When the school year was over in December, he headed home for several weeks. Camp began in February.

Luis' mother was excited about the idea of her son being at a Christian camp. She told Luis, "I'm

MR. COHEN OFFERED TO PAY FOR THE CAMP.

not sure you are a real, born-again Christian."

Luis rolled his eyes around saying, "Mom, come on." But his mother knew the truth about her only son.

February finally arrived. Luis had never been to a camp, so he was excited to go to the mountainous area in southern Argentina. It was like the Scouts, with everyone sleeping in Argentine army tents and foldable cots. Fifty or sixty boys from St. Alban's school were there along with Mr. Cohen and several British and American counselors from different missionary organizations.

At the two-week camp, Luis received Bible lessons and memorized Bible verses along with the usual fun and games. There was no contact with the outside world, and Luis missed it. He felt totally cut off from life. He couldn't even learn the soccer scores, and soccer was as big in Argentina as football is in the United States.

IT WAS LIKE THE SCOUTS, SLEEPING IN ARGENTINE ARMY TENTS.

At the camp, Mr. Cohen, the normally stiff, curt, and formal teacher, changed into someone completely different. Luis was beginning to like camp, but he knew he couldn't get away from the one tradition at the camp that he dreaded. Each counselor had about ten boys in his tent. One boy was taken each night for a walk and given an opportunity to say yes or no to Christ's claims on his life.

Every night, Luis waited with a sick feeling in the pit of his stomach to be told that it was his turn to walk with Frank Chandler, his counselor. Every night, some other boy's name was called. Finally, every other boy in his tent had walked with Frank. Luis knew that this night would be his turn.

Even though Luis felt guilty for his sins, he didn't want to face the issue of his salvation. *Maybe I'll pretend to be asleep and Frank will go away,* Luis thought. The counselor came and shook Luis, but the boy continued pretending to be asleep. Finally, Frank dumped Luis on the ground.

EACH COUNSELOR HAD ABOUT TEN BOYS IN A TENT.

"Come on, Luis," Frank said. "Get up." The pair walked outside the tent and sat down on a fallen tree. A light rain was beginning to fall.

"Luis," Frank said, "are you a born-again Christian?"

"I don't think so," Luis said.

"It's not a matter of whether you think so or not. Are you or aren't you?" Frank persisted.

"No, I'm not," Luis said slowly.

"If you died tonight," Frank asked Luis, "would you go to heaven or hell?"

For a moment, Luis sat quietly and thought about his answer, "I'm going to hell."

"Is that where you want to go?"

"No," Luis said.

"Then why are you going there?" Frank asked.

With a shrug of his shoulders, Luis said, "I don't know."

Frank flipped open the pages of his Bible and read from the Apostle Paul's letter to the Romans

FRANK SAID: "ARE YOU A BORN-AGAIN CHRISTIAN?"

using Luis' name: "If you confess with your lips, Luis, that Jesus is Lord, and believe in your heart that God raised him from the dead, you, Luis, will be saved. For man believes with his heart and so is justified, and he confesses with his lips and so is saved" (Romans 10:9-10, RSV).

After reading, Frank looked up and said, "Luis, do you believe in your heart that God raised Jesus from the dead?"

"Yes, I do," Luis said.

"Then what do you have to do next to be saved?"

As it began to rain even harder, Luis hesitated. Frank re-read verse 9: " 'If you confess with your lips that Jesus is Lord. . .you will be saved.' "

"Luis, are you ready to confess Jesus as your Lord right now?"

"Yes."

"All right, let's pray." Frank put his arm around Luis' shoulder and led him in a prayer.

"ALL RIGHT, LET'S PRAY."

Luis prayed, "Lord Jesus, I believe You were raised from the dead. I confess You with my lips. Give me eternal life. I want to be Yours. Save me from hell. Amen."

After the prayer, Luis began to cry. He gave Frank a big hug; then they ran back to the tent. When Luis crawled under his blanket, he pulled out his flashlight and wrote two lines in his Bible: "February 12, 1947" and "I received Jesus Christ."

At age twelve, Luis Palau knew he was a member of God's family. "When compared to eternal life with Christ, every other decision seems unimportant," Luis said later.

When Luis returned home and told his mother, she was ecstatic. The excitement about his decision lasted for several months. While not obnoxious about his faith, Luis began to carry his Bible often and became more active in the Crusaders youth group at school.

Because of the time he spent with Mr. Cohen at

"FEBRUARY 12, 1947, I RECEIVED JESUS CHRIST."

camp, Luis felt close to his teacher. He pitched in to help with the Crusaders youth group meetings held in the Cohen home Sunday afternoons. Some of his friends at school didn't know how to accept Luis' increased Christian activity.

As time passed, Luis started to have less excitement about Christ. He wasn't sure what the reason was. Maybe it was the constant pressure from his friends at school to listen to soccer matches and attend movies. Whatever the reason, while he continued to be active in Christian activities, Luis' initial excitement about the Gospel began to dim.

One day when Luis returned to school from a Crusaders meeting, he carelessly left his Bible on a streetcar and lost it. Without a copy of the Bible, Luis quickly lost his enthusiasm over Bible classes and almost anything else concerning his commitment to Christ.

One day Luis was showing off in art class. Mr. Thompson, the new art teacher, walked over and

HE CARELESSLY LEFT HIS BIBLE ON A STREETCAR.

made a sarcastic remark about Luis' horrible painting of a tree. Luis knew the painting was bad. As the teacher turned and walked away, Luis spat out a foul word in Spanish. Since Mr. Thompson had recently come from England, Luis figured the teacher wouldn't know the word. But the other students understood and roared with laughter.

"What did you say, Palau?" the teacher asked.

"Oh, nothing, Mr. Thompson, sir. Nothing, really."

"No, what was it, Palau?"

"It was really nothing important, sir."

"I'd really like to hear it again, Palau. Would you mind repeating it?"

"Oh, I don't think it's worth repeating. I—"

"All right," Mr. Thompson snapped. "Go see the master on duty."

The class was stunned. At St. Alban's, to see the master on duty was the ultimate form of punishment. The fearful role of disciplinarian rotated

THE OTHER STUDENTS UNDERSTOOD AND ROARED WITH LAUGHTER.

among the professors. No one tells the master on duty why the student has come for punishment. The student must tell the master himself, then take whatever punishment is given. Luis cringed when he saw that Mr. Cohen was the master on duty.

"Come in, Palau," Mr. Cohen said. "Why are you here?"

"Mr. Thompson sent me."

"Is that so? Why?"

For someone who Luis had spent a lot of time with in Crusaders meetings and summer camp, Mr. Cohen acted terribly cold and distant.

"Well, I said a bad word," Luis confessed.

"Repeat it," Mr. Cohen directed.

"Oh, I had better not," Luis said.

"Repeat it," the teacher insisted.

Luis hung his head and repeated the word from art class. The teacher sat and stared in disappointment at Luis. Then he reached around for his cricket bat.

"REPEAT IT," THE TEACHER INSISTED.

"You know, Palau, I'm going to give you six of the best," he said. It was the maximum amount of punishment.

"Bend and touch your toes, please," Mr. Cohen said. "Before I punish you, I want to tell you this, Palau. You are the greatest hypocrite I have ever seen in my life."

Luis winced at the strong words.

"You think you get away with your arrogant, cynical, above-it-all, know-it-all attitude, but I have watched you. You come to Bible class, all right, but you are a hypocrite."

The physical punishment stung for days. It hurt horribly whenever Luis had to sit down. He slept on his stomach for a week. For the next several months, Luis hated Mr. Cohen. He quit attending the Crusaders meetings and didn't pay any attention during Bible classes. At church services, Luis walked through the motions but tuned out any teaching.

Luis' relationship with God was broken. Luis

"PALAU, YOU ARE THE GREATEST HYPOCRITE I HAVE EVER SEEN."

turned to school dances and reading magazines about car racing and sports on Sunday. He quickly became a fast-talking, smooth-working phony. He chose non-Christian kids for friends. They did what Luis had been taught were sins—going to soccer games on Sundays, wasting time and fantasizing about girls. He never talked with these friends about Christ or what the Lord could do for their lives. Instead, Luis went along with the crowd and their activities—until Carnival Week.

THEY DID WHAT LUIS HAD BEEN TAUGHT WERE SINS.

IF LUIS GOT INVOLVED IN CARNIVAL WEEK,
HE COULD CUT HIS TIES WITH CHRISTIANITY.

3

In many South American countries, the week before Lent is marked with wild abandonment. In Argentina, it's called Carnival Week. Most businesses close for the entire week, and just about any kind of behavior is allowed.

Luis had grown tired of the little parties and games from past years. He decided that if he got involved in Carnival Week events, he could firmly cut his ties with Christianity.

Luis' friends planned to pick him up for the first day of the week-long celebration. He knew many of the activities were wrong, so the night before he fell to his knees beside his bed and pleaded with God, "Get me out of this, and I will give up everything that's of the world. I will serve You and give my whole life to You. Just get me out of this!"

Sometimes God answers prayer in amazing ways! The next morning Luis slowly sat up and noticed his mouth felt strange. Stumbling to a mirror, Luis saw that he looked like he had swallowed a ping-pong ball. Then Luis managed a crooked smile in the mirror. Out loud he said, "God has answered my prayer!"

On the telephone, Luis reached one of his friends, "I can't go to the dance tonight, and I won't be going to the carnival all this week."

"Come on, Luis!" the friend protested. "Everything has been planned!"

"I WILL SERVE YOU AND GIVE YOU MY WHOLE LIFE."

"No," Luis said. "I have a good reason, and I will not go."

"I'm coming over," he insisted. "You must be crazy."

A few minutes later, the young man arrived with three or four other friends, but Luis had made up his mind not to attend Carnival Week. His friends left, admitting defeat. Firm in his decision, Luis walked inside, determined to destroy the things that kept him from following Jesus. He tore up his university club membership card and ripped up his soccer and car-racing magazines. He also tossed out many record albums.

The next day, Luis went to church morning and night. While the rest of his town was caught up in the merry-making of Carnival Week, Luis returned to the Lord.

Having repaired his relationship with God, Luis needed to decide what to do with the rest of his life. Since he was finished with school, he decided it

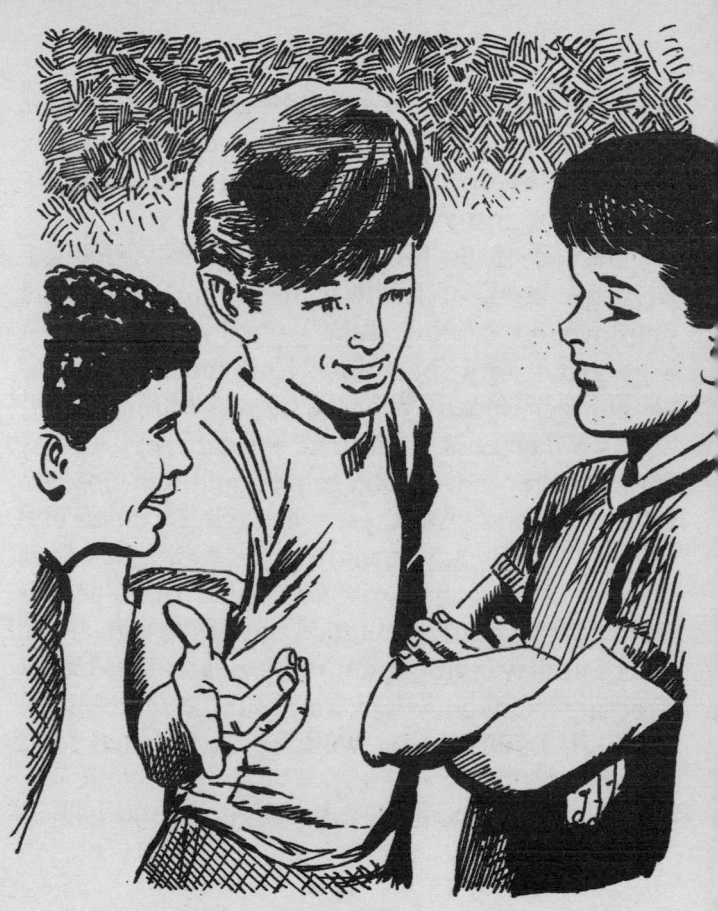

LUIS HAD MADE UP HIS MIND NOT TO ATTEND CARNIVAL WEEK.

was time to begin a career. Although he was only in his mid-teens, Luis lived in a time and place where boys were expected to take on serious responsibilities at a young age.

Because Luis had a bilingual British education, the Bank of London hired him as a junior employee-in-training. Luis gained a reputation as a go-getter. In a short time, Luis received several promotions, mostly because he was bilingual.

One day Luis submitted some papers, asking for a transfer to Cordoba so he could live closer to his mother and sisters. He was taking a much bigger risk than it may seem. No one ever asked for a transfer in the bank Luis worked at. To do so was to risk being fired or laughed out of the office. But Luis felt it was important to be nearer his family. Trusting that God would work out the situation for the best, Luis kept on working and waited for a response.

One day, Luis received a memo asking him to

THE BANK OF LONDON HIRED LUIS AS AN EMPLOYEE-IN-TRAINING.

report to the personnel office. Full of fear, he walked to the office.

"Why do you want to transfer to Cordoba?" the personnel manager asked Luis.

"My mother and sisters live there. In addition, I know the bank has a good branch in the city," Luis said.

An uncomfortable silence filled the room.

"You know," the manager said, "it would be good for you. In a branch of that size, you can learn banking more quickly since only one or two people are in each major department. In fact, we'll put this down as if it were our idea. Then we can justify paying for your move and giving you a promotion and raise."

Luis felt stunned. The manager continued, "If you progress as nicely there as you have here at headquarters, within six months we'll put you in charge of foreign operations of that branch, and in a year we'll bring you back here for a few weeks of

"WHY DO YOU WANT TO TRANSFER TO CORDOBA?"

specialized training. In our eyes, you will begin as the number four man in Cordoba." Luis hadn't reached his eighteenth birthday.

Time passed quickly as Luis' move was approved and he gathered his belongings. His sisters and mother were excited to learn that he would once again be near home.

A few weeks before his move to Cordoba, Luis was lying on the living room floor at his Uncle Arnold and Aunt Marjorie's home. Luis tuned in a shortwave radio program from HCJB in Quito, Ecuador. He didn't catch the preacher's name, but Luis heard him calling men to come to Jesus Christ. Later, he realized that he had been listening to Billy Graham. On that living room floor, Luis prayed, "Jesus, someday use me on the radio to bring others to You, just as this program has firmed up my resolve to completely live for You."

Soon Luis was settled in Cordoba. He became involved in a church, and when he was eighteen

"JESUS, SOMEDAY, USE ME ON THE RADIO."

years old, he taught a Sunday school class of young boys. One of the members of his class faced a family crisis—his parents were separated. Divorce wasn't common in Argentina at that time, and any sign of marriage problems was frowned on. The boy was having a hard time adjusting to his family situation and the unkind comments people made.

The boy listened intently when Luis taught the class, but he never spoke. Later that week, Luis visited the boy at his grandmother's house and led him into a personal relationship with Christ.

The next week, the boy wasn't in class, so Luis went to see his grandmother. She told him the story. After accepting Christ, the boy was riding his bike and grabbed hold of a street car. The bike slipped under the wheels of the street car and the youngster was killed instantly.

The grandmother told Luis, "My grandson is in heaven now, and we are at peace." Luis learned to

HE TAUGHT A SUNDAY SCHOOL CLASS OF YOUNG BOYS.

speak for Christ whenever God opened the door of opportunity.

Throughout this time of his life, Luis had one central thought: Take care of your family. Over the years, his mother's financial situation had gotten worse. Luis lived with his four sisters and mother in a small house. Even with his job, there wasn't enough money to provide for six adults. Some nights, the family supper amounted to a loaf of French bread with some garlic flavoring. The family never complained about the slim meals. Often during the brief meal, Mrs. Palau read from a devotional book such as Charles Spurgeon's *Checkbook of Faith*.

At the bank, Luis' co-workers began to call him pastor. He used his free time at work for Bible study. He still dreamed of being an evangelist. While Luis studied, prayed, taught, and witnessed, he saw few results from his efforts.

Luis read the stories of great evangelists and

SOME NIGHTS, THE FAMILY SUPPER AMOUNTED TO A LOAF OF FRENCH BREAD.

was excited about how they were used by God in people's lives. Yet it seemed obvious to Luis that he didn't have whatever the gift was that they had. Finally Luis gave God a deadline. *If I don't see any converts by the end of this year, Lord, then I'll quit preaching,* Luis prayed. The end of the year arrived without any changes. Luis decided God must have something different for him to do.

About four days into the new year, Luis purchased a Spanish version of Billy Graham's *The Secret of Happiness*. He curled up on the couch to study the book. Despite his low feelings about his evangelism and service to God, Luis was encouraged by Billy Graham's thoughts about the Beatitudes from the Sermon on the Mount in Matthew 5. While reading, he memorized the major points for each Beatitude.

That evening, Luis thought about skipping the home Bible study, but out of loyalty to the elders, he caught the bus to the meeting. After several hymns,

LUIS PURCHASED A SPANISH VERSION OF BILLY GRAHAM'S BOOK, *THE SECRET OF HAPPINESS.*

the speaker still hadn't arrived. The host said, "Luis, you're going to have to speak. None of the other preachers are here."

Luis protested, "I'm not prepared, and besides I didn't bring my Bible."

The host wouldn't be deterred. "Look, Luis, there's no one else. You have to speak."

With hardly time to breathe a prayer, Luis borrowed a New Testament and turned to Matthew 5. He read a Beatitude, then repeated a few points from Billy Graham's book. After several verses, he reached the Beatitude, "Blessed are the pure in heart, for they shall see God" (Matthew 5:8, RSV).

Suddenly a woman stood and began to cry, "Somebody help me! My heart is not pure. How am I going to find God?"

Luis told everyone to turn to 1 John 1:7 where they read, "The blood of Jesus, his Son, purifies us from all sin." He explained God's plan of salvation, and the woman discovered peace with God.

"MY HEART IS NOT PURE. HOW AM I GOING TO FIND GOD?"

That evening, Luis learned some important lessons. It wasn't his job to convict people of sin. The Holy Spirit did that. Luis was the vehicle God used to lead the repentant woman to Christ. Perhaps Luis could be an evangelist after all.

Luis began to dream about mass evangelism where hundreds and thousands of people could be won to Christ. As Luis prayed and read about mass evangelism, he became certain of one thing: He didn't want to be involved in such crusades if his purpose was to get a great reputation. From the beginning, Luis sensed that if his ego got out of hand, the Lord would quickly put him in his place. So he simply prayed, "Lord, please make everything I do pleasing to You." Luis shifted his personal study into high gear.

One day in late 1958, Luis received a flier announcing a meeting with two Americans: Dick Hillis, a former missionary to China, and Ray Stedman, a pastor from Palo Alto, California. At the

"LORD, PLEASE MAKE EVERYTHING I DO PLEASING TO YOU."

meeting, speaking English, Luis introduced himself to Pastor Stedman.

Pastor Stedman asked Luis many questions and was genuinely interested in the answers. Luis was flattered when Pastor Stedman invited him to a Bible study with a few missionaries the next morning.

After the Bible study, Pastor Stedman needed to shop in town, so Luis gave him a ride on his motorbike. "Would you like to go to seminary?" Pastor Stedman asked.

"It would be nice, but I'm not sure I'll ever make it," Luis answered. "I don't have a lot of money, and my church doesn't encourage formal theological education."

"Well," Pastor Stedman said, "it could be arranged if the Lord wanted it. How would you like to come to the United States?"

"I've thought about it," Luis admitted. "Maybe someday I'll be able to go, the Lord willing." He thought the conversation was simply about dreams.

"HOW WOULD YOU LIKE TO COME TO THE UNITED STATES?"

"You know, Luis," Stedman said, "the Lord may just will it."

The next night, Luis took Dick Hillis and Ray Stedman to the airport. "I'll see you in the United States," Pastor Stedman promised.

"Well, the Lord willing, maybe someday," Luis said.

"No, Luis, the Lord is going to will. I'll write you from the plane."

As Luis left the airport, he thought about Ray Stedman. The man seemed warm and flattering, yet a bit unrealistic. Why bother to dream?

A few days later, Ray's letter arrived with the news that he knew a businessman who wanted to finance Luis' trip to the United States so that Luis could study at Dallas Theological Seminary. At first, Luis found the news thrilling, but then he changed his mind because so many people in Argentina needed the Good News about Jesus. He didn't want to spend four years in seminary, and

"I'LL SEE YOU IN THE UNITED STATES."

who would take care of his family? He wrote Stedman and declined his offer.

Immediately, Stedman wrote again, assuring Luis that someone from the United States would also provide for the needs of his family. The opportunity seemed too incredible, so Luis put off answering for several months. Although Luis knew it was rude not to answer, he ignored a couple more letters.

Things were also changing at the bank. One day Luis confronted the bank manager about some new policies. Because of his Christian testimony, Luis told the manager that he couldn't meet the requirements for his job with a clear conscience. The practices weren't illegal, but they raised ethical questions. The manager reminded Luis about how much the bank had done for him and what they planned for his future. Luis didn't back down. After that conversation, he could feel a change in atmosphere at the bank.

One day at work, Luis met Keith Bentson, who

BECAUSE OF HIS CHRISTIAN TESTIMONY,
LUIS COULDN'T MEET THE REQUIREMENTS OF THE BANK.

worked at SEPAL, the Latin American division of a company named OC International. Keith was looking for a Christian to translate English material into Spanish. Luis jumped at the opportunity to change jobs—even though it meant a cut in his pay.

While at SEPAL, Luis continued holding evangelistic tent meetings throughout the city of Cordoba. He dreamed of pulling together a team of people to conduct crusades, but had no idea how that would happen because his money was too tight to hire anyone.

One night after a meeting, an American, Bruce Woodman, introduced himself to Luis and asked if he wanted a soloist or a song leader for his meetings. Luis instantly agreed to add Bruce to the team as well as Bill Fasig, who could play either the organ or piano for meetings. A team was born.

LUIS HELD EVANGELISTIC TENT MEETINGS.

UNANSWERED LETTERS GREW MORE URGENT, YET LUIS DIDN'T RESPOND TO THEM.

4

The excitement of evangelistic meetings and working for SEPAL gave Luis one more excuse for not answering Ray Stedman's letters. Pastor Stedman continued to invite Luis to go to the United States and get additional training. His unanswered letters grew more urgent, yet Luis didn't respond to them.

Finally, Pastor Stedman wrote a stinging letter that said the inaction from Luis was rude and irresponsible. In spite of Luis' failure to respond to his

LUIS PALAU

letters, Stedman made it clear that if he wanted, Luis could still come to the United States. Stedman encouraged Luis to study at Dallas Theological Seminary, but also said Luis wouldn't be forced to study there or anywhere else for four years.

"Too many people are going to hell for me to be spending four more years reading books," Luis wrote in a letter to Pastor Stedman. "I can study at home. I'm disciplined, and I enjoy studying. What I need is an opportunity to ask questions of some good Bible teachers and get answers to the really tough ones I haven't been able to resolve through my own reading."

Ray Stedman told Luis about a one-year graduate course in theology at Multnomah Biblical Seminary in Portland, Oregon. He also offered an internship for Luis in his California church before and after the school year. Then Pastor Stedman sent money for Luis' mother to reassure him that support would continue while Luis was in the United States.

"WHAT I NEED IS AN OPPORTUNITY TO ASK QUESTIONS OF SOME GOOD BIBLE TEACHERS."

Pastor Stedman also enclosed a check so Luis could travel to Buenos Aires and get his passport. Every excuse was covered. For a long time, Luis had wanted to go to the United States. So he prayed about going, and agreed to come to California.

A small crowd of family and friends gathered with Luis Palau at the Ezeiza International Airport in Buenos Aires. Luis was traveling to the United States on the first airline flight of his life. During the tearful farewell, his mother just couldn't get in enough last minute advice.

She said, "Don't go into the cities; don't travel alone; watch out; don't get shot and stuffed into a trunk, and remember Hebrews 13:5 and 6!" She was worried about murder, but Luis was worried about the trip. The pair hugged in the airport, and Luis turned to go. Luis was wearing his only brand-new, black suit.

The old DC-6 chugged over the Andes mountains, then settled into a lower altitude to take the

THE OLD D-C 6 CHUGGED OVER THE ANDES MOUNTAINS.

strain off the engines. Every time the plane climbed or suddenly dropped in altitude, Luis had a stomachache. Luis stared out the window, and said in his best English, "Look at all those little white boats."

His seat mate rose and leaned across to look. "Those are clouds, kid," he said in a bored tone of voice.

The flight reached Miami ten hours late, so Luis missed his connecting flight. He was exhausted. His new suit looked rumpled, and Luis was worried. Three thousand miles away, Ray Stedman was expecting him to speak in his church.

After a collect call to Pastor Stedman and a sorry attempt at a few hours of sleep, Luis was on a Delta jet headed to San Francisco. Luis could not believe the airline. Delta gave away many free cups of coffee, sugar, plastic spoons, maps, and post-cards. *This must be the land of opportunity,* Luis thought.

As the jet moved across the nation, it stopped in

"THOSE ARE CLOUDS, KID."

cities like Atlanta. *Someday we'll have evangelistic crusades here*, Luis thought. It was only a dream. Luis had never seen a crusade, let alone preached at one, but in his heart, he felt a burden from God. It was only a matter of time. The first step would take place in California. The plane landed, and Luis began a new life.

"Luis, stay with me everywhere I go," Ray Stedman said as Luis began his internship at Palo Alto Bible Church. "It's the best way for you to learn."

The pastor's calendar was full of counseling appointments. Through every session, Luis sat in the corner behind the counselee. "Don't worry about Luis," Pastor Stedman told the counselee. "He's just learning." Soon the person forgot about Palau sitting in the corner of the room. Luis watched the pastor work with people.

One day, Bob, a member of the church, asked for an appointment. Luis dreaded sitting through that meeting because Bob consistently caused trouble for

"LUIS, STAY WITH ME EVERYWHERE I GO."

Pastor Stedman. *What will happen during this session?* Luis wondered.

"I'm here to give you some money for the church," Bob began, pulling out a check for $15,000 and giving it to the pastor. The Palo Alto Bible Church was booming and could certainly use the unexpected gift.

As Luis watched, Pastor Stedman walked over to Bob, picked up the check, and tore it into small pieces. "I don't care about your money, Bob," the pastor said. "I care about your soul. You're not going to buy my affection. You need to give your life to Jesus Christ."

After Bob walked out of the room, Luis asked Pastor Stedman, "How are you able to go so fast and decide so quickly what is the heart of the issue?"

"Never speak to the mask," Ray Stedman explained. "Everyone wears a mask about their true problem, but you need to get behind the mask."

Pastor Stedman cut through false piety and

PASTOR STEDMAN TORE THE CHECK INTO SMALL PIECES.

emphasized a commitment to the Bible for every action. It was an important lesson that would help Luis with his counseling in the years ahead.

Two months with the Stedman family was hardly enough time for Luis to plunge into American culture. He needed to learn how to eat and behave like other people in the country. But it was all the time he had before traveling north to Multnomah Biblical Seminary in Portland, Oregon.

In his first term at Multnomah, Luis found his studies were a challenge. While he had done a lot of reading and studying, Luis knew little about some of the more technical areas of study he now faced. Sometimes Luis felt frustrated not to be able to live with joy, release, and freedom like Ray Stedman and several other Christians he had met. The more Luis desired a deeper life with Christ, the more it seemed to elude him.

The other students and faculty at Multnomah treated Luis royally. To them, Luis looked like a

THE STUDENTS AND FACULTY AT MULTNOMAH TREATED LUIS ROYALLY.

friendly, winsome, and somewhat different South American. Unknown to them, Luis faced discouragement and spiritual battles. If Luis hadn't cared so much about his service to Christ and preaching the Gospel, he might have given up during the first term and gone back to Argentina.

Luis reached a new low around Thanksgiving. The second term would start in only a month. Luis felt it was a hopeless dream to be able to attend. A friend at Ray Stedman's church had paid for his first term, but Luis had no money for the rest of the year. *As soon as the term is over, I'm going back to Argentina,* Luis decided.

That weekend, Luis checked his mailbox for a letter from home. The only thing in the box was a plain envelope with his name on it. The teachers used the mailboxes for returning graded papers, so Luis assumed another assignment was in the envelope. When he pulled the paper out, Luis saw a simple typewritten letter without any

THE ONLY THING IN THE BOX WAS AN ENVELOPE WITH HIS NAME ON IT.

identification or signature. It read:

> *Dear Luis,*
> *You have been a great blessing to many*
> *of us here in the States, and we appre-*
> *ciate what you have taught us. We feel*
> *that you deserve help to finish your*
> *year at Multnomah; therefore, all your*
> *tuition and books have been paid for.*
>
> *Just check in at the business office,*
> *and they will finalize the papers. So*
> *you will be grateful to every American*
> *you have met or will ever meet, we*
> *remain anonymous.*

So God is still with me after all! Luis thought.

During that year, Luis developed a growing interest in a member of his class—Patricia Scofield. One evening, Luis and several others went to a class party. Luis asked Pat, "May I walk you over?"

"MAY I WALK YOU OVER?"

She said, "Sure." It was no big deal, and they weren't even together at the party. But Luis became interested. To Luis, Pat seemed mature and smart—and she knew how to dress well. As they talked, Luis learned that Pat was spiritually sensitive. As he walked across the campus to his classes, Luis began to keep an eye out for Pat.

TO LUIS, PAT SEEMED MATURE AND SMART—
AND SHE KNEW HOW TO DRESS WELL.

DR. KEHOE BEGAN EACH CLASS BY QUOTING GALATIANS 2:20.

5

Luis grew more and more discouraged about his spiritual life. He was taking a course called Spiritual Life, taught by Dr. George Kehoe. Dr. Kehoe began each class by quoting Galatians 2:20: "I have been crucified with Christ and I no longer live, but Christ lives in me. The life I live in the body, I live by faith in the Son of God, who loved me and gave himself for me."

The verse was a gnawing reminder to Luis of

the lack of fruit in his spiritual life. He was frustrated at his failure. If asked to describe himself, Luis would have said that he was envious, jealous, preoccupied, self-centered, and overly ambitious.

Shortly before Christmas break, Major Ian Thomas spoke at the Multnomah chapel service. Luis had begun sitting in the back of the auditorium during chapel services. Usually the chapel services were another dose of exposition or missionary stories. In the back of the room, he dared the speaker to make him pay attention. If the speaker was good, he then honored him by listening. Otherwise, Luis daydreamed or peeked at his class notes.

Major Thomas was founder and general director of the Torchbearers, the group that runs the Capernwray Hall Bible School in England. His British accent and staccato delivery were unusual, but what really intrigued Luis was the way Thomas pointed with a partially amputated finger. Thomas' twenty-two minute message brought

MAJOR THOMAS POINTED WITH A PARTIALLY AMPUTATED FINGER.

some dramatic changes for Palau.

Ian Thomas talked about Moses spending forty years in the wilderness to learn that he was nothing. Then one day, Moses was confronted with a burning bush. Thomas said that the burning bush was likely a dry bunch of ugly little sticks that had hardly developed, yet Moses had to take off his shoes. Why? Because this was holy ground. God was in the bush! God was telling Moses, "I don't need a pretty bush or an educated bush or an eloquent bush. Any old bush will do, as long as I am in the bush. If I am going to use you, I am going to use you. It will not be you doing something for Me, but Me doing something through you."

The illustration hit Luis in a fresh way. He was that type of bush: a worthless, useless bunch of dried-up sticks. Palau could do nothing for God. All of his reading, studying, asking questions, and trying to model himself after others was worthless—unless God was in the bush. And only God could

THIS WAS HOLY GROUND. GOD WAS IN THE BUSH!

make something happen.

To close his message, Thomas read Galatians 2:20. All at once, Luis understood the passage. "I have been crucified with Christ and I no longer live, but Christ lives in me." His biggest spiritual struggle was finally over! He decided to let God be God and then let Luis Palau depend on Him.

A tremendous spiritual release flooded Luis. He ran back to his room, and in tears, fell to his knees next to his bunk. He prayed in Spanish, "Lord, now I understand! The whole thing is 'not I, but Christ in me.' It's not what I'm going to do for You but rather what You are going to do through me."

For the next hour and a half, Luis stayed on his knees and continued praying. He asked God to forgive his pride. *Oh, I was really something, but God was not active in the bush. I hadn't given Him a chance.* Luis allowed God to take control of his life.

That day marked a turning point in Luis' spiritual life. The practical working out of that discovery

HE DECIDED TO LET GOD BE GOD AND THEN LET LUIS PALAU DEPEND ON HIM.

would be lengthy and painful, but at last the realization had come. Luis could begin to relax and rest in Jesus.

In the meantime, Luis began to get better acquainted with Pat Scofield outside of class. By Valentine's Day, they were unofficially engaged. A quick meeting with the college president allowed them to make it official a few days later.

Not long after that, Pat noticed that Luis seemed to be a bit reluctant to talk about their upcoming marriage. "Luis, my dad has been figuring out how to get enough money to pay for our wedding," Pat said.

"Pay for the wedding?" Luis repeated. "What does that mean?"

"It's the custom that the parents of the bride pay for the wedding," Pat explained.

"Everything?" Luis asked, his tone rising in excitement.

"Of course—except for possibly the reception

"IT'S THE CUSTOM THAT THE PARENTS OF THE BRIDE
PAY FOR THE WEDDING."

dinner, and we can go simple on that," Pat added.

Relief passed across Luis' face. "Then what are we waiting for?"

Luis had known his finances were incredibly tight. His mother and sisters couldn't afford to pay for anything to do with the wedding. In Argentina, the couples split the expenses fifty/fifty. Luis was glad to learn the custom was different in America!

At the end of the school year, Luis headed back to Palo Alto to continue his internship with Ray Stedman, while Pat stayed in Portland. For two long months, the couple wrote letters. They had no money for phone calls. In one of these letters, Luis wrote Pat about a conversation with one of the elders, Bob Connell.

Throughout his internship, Luis had not told anyone about the secret dreams of his heart—evangelism and evangelistic crusades.

One day Bob had pulled Luis aside and said, "Luis, I believe God is going to use you to win as

FOR TWO LONG MONTHS, THE COUPLE WROTE LETTERS.

many souls as Billy Graham—even in this country." Luis didn't know what to say in response.

After completing his internship, Luis raced back up the coast in an old '55 Buick he bought from Ray Stedman. He arrived in Portland just a few days before the wedding. On August 5, 1961, Pastor Wollen and Ray Stedman officiated Luis and Pat's marriage.

After a two-week honeymoon, the Palaus drove back to the San Francisco Bay area. After they were interviewed by the OC International board, the Palaus were accepted for missionary service. Then they drove back to Portland and packed for their missionary internship in Detroit.

"America the free." The words meant something to Luis. From his first days in the U.S., he loved the freedom to travel and the cleanliness and order of the society. But each January, Luis had to register again with the U.S. government. He constantly lived with the fear that if he made a mistake of any

THE PALAUS DROVE BACK TO THE SAN FRANCISCO BAY AREA.

kind, he would be shipped back to Argentina on the first Pan American flight out of the country.

After his marriage to Pat, Luis applied to become an American citizen. It was not a simple process. He had to learn the Preamble to the United States Constitution, the Pledge of Allegiance, and take an examination. Then he appeared in front of a United States judge and renounced any allegiance to Argentina and his citizenship in that country. He was embracing America and found the experience invigorating— almost like a conversion.

Immediately after the ceremony, Luis climbed into his old Buick and drove to a bridge along the Old Bayshore Freeway. He parked his car and leaned over the bridge. In his hand, Luis had his old green card. The document gave him permission to live and work in the United States even though he wasn't a citizen. He no longer needed it. *Rip!* Luis tore it into tiny pieces and tossed it off the bridge. As the green pieces of paper fluttered down into the

HE APPEARED IN FRONT OF A UNITED STATES JUDGE.

bay, he shouted, "I'm an American! Nobody can kick me out of this country!"

Besides becoming an American, Luis reached another milestone that summer of 1962—Pat discovered she was pregnant. Luis was going to be a father.

"I'M AN AMERICAN!"

PAT SUDDENLY ANNOUNCED IT WAS TIME TO GO TO THE HOSPITAL.

6

In January 1963, Pat was seven months pregnant. While doing missionary fund-raising work at Valley Church in Cupertino, California, the Palaus were staying in the home of some friends. Pat suddenly announced it was time to go to the hospital. Luis couldn't believe it. He reminded Pat about their plan for their first child—to return home to Portland in two months. The baby couldn't come now.

"Tell that to the baby," Pat said.

They headed to Stanford University Hospital. After Luis had been waiting for more than an hour in the hallway, the doctor, a Christian friend from Palo Alto, came and said there were serious complications. Luis paced the hallway and after several hours, assumed the baby had been lost, or the doctor would have returned. Then the doctor walked down the hall with a huge grin.

"Congratulations!" he said. "You're the father of twin boys!" Kevin and Keith were premature and weighed less than four pounds each. They stayed in the hospital for five weeks before finally they were brought home.

The rest of the year was busy as the Palaus adjusted to having doubled their family's size. Later that year, Luis was ordained at Ray Stedman's church. Then the Palaus flew to Costa Rica, where they were going to attend language school. It was Pat's first time outside of the U.S. The

"YOU'RE THE FATHER OF TWIN BOYS!"

twins weren't quite a year old. Pat cried because of the overwhelming adjustments, but several students who attended the language school with the Palaus created a fun Christmas that year to help ease the cultural shock.

During the summer of 1964, the Palaus arrived in Bogotá, Colombia. As new missionaries, their assignment was training men and women in evangelism and church planting. Luis and several others held Colombia's first evangelistic street meetings after a decade of violent persecutions and killings. The Palaus and others felt change was in the air for Colombia.

Later that year, Luis and several others flew back to Quito, Ecuador. They were going to launch a new evangelistic concept on television. At HCJB, Luis opened the telephone lines for live counseling television broadcasts with the potential to reach large numbers of people for Christ.

Initially, they started with a short program but

SEVERAL STUDENTS AT THE LANGUAGE SCHOOL
CREATED A FUN CHRISTMAS.

long after it went off the air, people continued to call the station. After a couple weeks, they were on the air for three hours at a time. Luis found the experience both invigorating and exhausting. The Lord had given him the ability to think quickly under pressure, but the program required rapid recall of specific passages from the Bible. Luis was forced to study the Bible with renewed vengeance. He had to store up God's answers for difficult problems in life.

Once the program went on the air, Luis never knew what to expect. One person would call who was on the verge of suicide; the next caller would be going through a messy divorce.

One night, Luis received two phone calls in a row. The first conversation was one of the most rewarding he had while working on the program, and the second turned into one of the most bizarre encounters of his ministry.

The first caller was a young flight attendant.

ONCE THE TV PROGRAM WENT ON THE AIR,
LUIS NEVER KNEW WHAT TO EXPECT.

She had sinned deeply and felt miserable, repentant, and desperate to be forgiven.

Until that evening, Luis had not led callers to Christ on the air. Instead, he counseled them from the Scriptures and set up an in-person appointment the next day. In the studio counseling office, he could carefully show them the way of salvation. But when this desperate caller heard Luis read from the Bible about God's offer of forgiveness and salvation, she wanted to receive Christ immediately. He hesitated and thought, *Would it look like a setup? This woman is obviously sincere about her decision.*

Luis asked her to pray with him, then added that anyone else watching by television who wanted to pray along with them and receive Christ could do so. "Dear God," he began, "I know I am a sinner." She repeated each line.

Luis and the woman prayed on and recounted what she had already explained through the phone

LUIS READ FROM THE BIBLE ABOUT GOD'S FORGIVENESS AND SALVATION.

call. "Father, I need Your forgiveness and Your saving love." As she prayed to receive Christ, Luis experienced a tearful, solemn moment. The young woman who trusted Christ on the air insisted on an appointment the next morning at nine.

The next caller was brief. A tiny, high-pitched, squeaky voice simply asked for an appointment the next day at nine-thirty. There was no more conversation. When Luis agreed to the time, the squeaky voice simply thanked him and hung up.

The next morning, Luis encouraged the young flight attendant in her new-found faith. As he walked her to the door and gave her a Bible and some literature, Luis noticed a little woman walking through the gates of the HCJB property. Two huge, able-bodied men walked close behind the woman. When she entered the office, Luis asked if the two gentlemen would like to come inside as well.

"No," she said, "one will stand by the door and the other by the gate." The person with the squeaky

LUIS NOTICED A LITTLE WOMAN WALKING THROUGH
THE GATES OF THE HCJB PROPERTY.

voice from the night before had arrived right on schedule. When she entered the room, she brushed past Luis and began to feel along the edges of the desk top as though she were searching for something. With no explanation, she moved to the wall and checked behind a hanging picture, then her eyes traveled to every corner of the room before she sat down.

She must be unbalanced, Luis thought.

As they talked, Luis became convinced the woman was unlike anyone he had ever met. She attacked each cigarette she took from her purse, sucking every last bit from it and lighting the next with the smoldering butt of the last one.

"You pastors and priests," she began with disgust. "You are a bunch of thieves and liars and crooks. All you want is to deceive people; all you want is money!" For more than twenty minutes, she continued with this type of talk. She swore constantly and accused and criticized. So

"YOU PASTORS AND PRIESTS ARE A BUNCH OF THIEVES AND LIARS."

much bitterness gushed from her that it left Luis speechless.

"Madam," Luis finally said, "is there anything I can do for you? How can I help you?"

She slowly took her cigarette from her lips and sat staring at Luis for an instant. Suddenly, she broke into uncontrollable sobs. After several minutes, Luis noticed the edge had disappeared from her voice. "You know," she said, "in the thirty-eight years I have lived, you are the first person who has ever asked me if he could help me."

"What is your name?" Luis asked.

Suddenly her tone changed and she looked hard again. "Why do you want to know my name?"

"Well, you've said a lot of things here, and I don't even know how to address you. I just want to know how to address you."

She shifted in her chair and sat straighter. "I'm going to tell you," she announced, as if allowing Luis to know her name was giving him a

"WHAT IS YOUR NAME?" LUIS ASKED.

privilege. "My name is Maria Benitez-Perez," she said triumphantly.

Luis recognized her last name as that of a large family of wealth and influence. "I am the secretary of the Communist Party here in Ecuador. I am a Marxist-Leninist, and I am a materialist. I don't believe in God."

For the next three hours, without pause or interruption, Maria talked. As a Marxist-Leninist, she made it quite clear that she opposed everything about Christianity. Luis continued listening and praying, *When will the opening come?*

"Listen, Palau," Maria finally said. "Supposing there is a God—and I'm not saying there is, because I don't believe the Bible, and I don't believe there's a God—but just supposing there is. Just for the sake of chatting about it, if there is a God—which there isn't—do you think He would receive a woman like me?"

So this little woman with the bold attitude had

"IF THERE IS A GOD—WOULD HE ACCEPT A WOMAN LIKE ME?"

a chink in her armor after all! Years before, Luis had studied Dr. R. A. Torrey's book, *How to Work for Christ*. He learned that when dealing with a professed atheist, the best approach is to take one verse from the Bible and stay with it, driving it home until it sticks, repeating it as many times as necessary. The Bible says that the law of the Lord converts the soul, Dr. Torrey wrote, not the arguments of men.

Which verse suits her? Luis wondered. As he prayed, the Lord reminded him of Hebrews 10:17, one of Luis' favorite verses: "Their sins and their lawless deeds I will remember no more" (NKJV).

Luis said, "Look, Maria, don't worry about what I think; look at what God thinks." He opened his Bible to the verse and let Maria read it.

"But I don't believe the Bi—"

"You've already told me that," Luis interrupted. "But we're just supposing there's a God, right? Let's just suppose this is His Word. He says,

"THEIR SINS AND THEIR LAWLESS DEEDS
I WILL REMEMBER NO MORE."

'Their sin and their lawless deeds I will remember no more.' "

She waited, as if she was expecting Luis to say more. He sat there in silence as she recounted a list of her sins.

Luis said, " 'Their sins and their lawless deeds I will remember no more.' " Internally, he began to count the times he repeated it.

"But I haven't told you half of my story. I stabbed a comrade who later committed suicide."

" 'Their sins and their lawless deeds I will remember no more.' "

"I've led student riots where people were killed!"

" 'Their sins and their lawless deeds I will remember no more.' "

"I egged on my friends and then hid while they were out dying for our cause."

" 'Their sins and their lawless deeds I will remember no more.' "

Seventeen times Luis responded to Maria's

"I'VE LED STUDENT RIOTS WHERE PEOPLE WERE KILLED!"

objections and confessions with that one Bible verse. It was past lunchtime. He felt tired and weak. "Would you like Christ to forgive all that you've told me about, and all the rest I don't even know?"

She was silent. Finally, she spoke softly and said, "If He could forgive me and change me, it would be the greatest miracle in the world." Luis led her in a simple prayer of commitment. By the end, she was crying.

A week later, Maria came back to HCJB and told Luis she was reading the Bible and felt a lot better. A longtime missionary from HCJB agreed to follow up on Maria, and Luis didn't see her again for two months.

In January 1966, a month before the Palaus' third son Andrew was born, Luis returned to Quito for more television counseling and radio program taping. While in Ecuador, Luis visited Maria and was shocked at her appearance because her face was a mess of purple blotches and bruises. Several

LUIS RETURNED TO QUITO FOR MORE TELEVISION COUNSELING
AND RADIO PROGRAM TAPING.

of her front teeth were missing.

After her last visit with Luis, Maria had told her comrades about her new faith during a meeting of all the communist leaders in the country. A few days later, a jeep full of her former comrades ran down Maria on the streets. The next day, several militant university students attacked her and smashed her face against a utility pole until she was unconscious. Maria was forced to hide out in the basements of several churches and in the homes of missionaries.

Luis listened to her story in amazement because she was such a young believer yet showed such courage. "There is going to be a revolution in June," she told Luis.

On the morning of the revolution, the Communist Party leader came out of hiding to talk with Maria. In a few hours, he was to become the new ruler of the country, but first he wanted to talk with his longtime friend.

MARIA HAD TOLD HER COMRADES ABOUT HER NEW FAITH.

"Maria," he asked, "why did you become a Christian?"

"Because I believe in God and in Jesus Christ, and my faith has changed my life."

"You know," he said, "while hiding out, I have been listening to HCJB radio on shortwave, and they almost have me believing there *is* a God!"

"There is!" she said. "Why don't you become a Christian and get out of this business! We never had any real convictions about atheism and materialism. And look at all the lives we've ruined and all the terrible things we've been into. Here, take this Bible and this book (*Peace with God* by Billy Graham). You can go to my father's farm and read them."

Miraculously, he accepted her offer. Later that morning, the disturbance fizzled into chaos, and Ecuador was saved from anarchy or tyranny.

Throughout the years, Luis had seen many people come to Christ, but Maria's was one of the most

"I BELIEVE IN GOD AND JESUS CHRIST."

dramatic stories. Yet, when Luis saw the effect of her conversion on the history of an entire country, it solidified his burden for the lost without Christ Jesus—not just for the good of individuals, but also for nations.

LUIS SAW THE EFFECT OF HER CONVERSION ON THE ENTIRE COUNTRY.

"BE PATIENT," WAS PASTOR STEDMAN'S ADVICE.

7

In Colombia, Luis was growing desperate to move into citywide evangelistic crusades. Although he didn't want to move away from OC International, he felt that maybe it would be necessary. Pastor Ray Stedman was in Guatemala for a pastor's conference and flew over to see Luis. "Be patient," was Pastor Stedman's advice.

"How long must I sit around and sit around?" Luis asked him. "If I have to leave OC and start on my own from scratch, I may do it."

"Be patient," Ray repeated. "If God is in it, it will happen when the time is right."

In late 1966, Luis prepared to attend the World Congress on Evangelism in Berlin. Just before leaving, he received some correspondence from Vic Whetzel, an OC board member. This man urged Luis to consider Mexico a fertile ground for mass evangelism. As Luis thought about the letter on the plane to Berlin, he wasn't sure what it meant.

One dark, cold afternoon when the congress meetings had let out early, many of the twelve hundred delegates were milling around West Berlin. Luis received a call from OC board members Dr. Ray Benson and Dr. Dick Hillis. The men wanted to take a walk with Luis and talk. They walked for a long time before they reached the point of their visit.

"Luis," Dick said, "we feel you and Pat should go home on furlough in December as planned.

"LUIS, WE FEEL YOU AND PAT SHOULD GO HOME
ON FURLOUGH IN DECEMBER."

Once your furlough is over, begin to develop your own evangelistic team with your sights set on Mexico. You'll be the field director for Mexico with your headquarters there."

For once, Luis stood speechless. A dream had come true. He was grateful for the patient work from his colleagues at OC International. Then Luis asked the two men for OC team member Joe Lathrop. Dick and Ray agreed readily and asked what else could be done. Luis said he would need someone for music, so they arranged for Bruce Woodman to work with him.

Before Luis left on furlough, the OC team held their first citywide crusade in Bogotá, Colombia. At the opening parade of the four-day crusade, thousands jammed the Bolivar Plaza. Even the president of Columbia came out of his office on the plaza and asked what was happening. By the time Luis spoke, twenty thousand people had jammed the plaza. Standing on the stairway of the main government

TWENTY THOUSAND PEOPLE HAD JAMMED THE PLAZA.

building, Luis preached on "Christ the Liberator" (John 8:36).

At the end of the brief message, three hundred people raised their hands, publicly committing their lives to Jesus Christ, and several hundred more were saved during the crusade meetings over the next four nights. With these four days, Luis Palau initiated a new era for mass evangelism throughout Latin America. He was eager to see what doors would open in Mexico for the Gospel of Jesus Christ.

During their work in Mexico, the Palau team heard about another religious group that had drawn a large crowd to a convention. For their next Mexico City crusade, the Palau team called it a convention. The response was overwhelming. In ten days, the crusade drew more than 106,000 people. Nearly 6,675 people committed their lives to Christ. Local churches in Mexico City doubled overnight.

LOCAL CHURCHES IN MEXICO CITY DOUBLED OVERNIGHT.

In many ways, the 1970 Mexico crusade was the spark that made many people focus their attention on mass evangelism south of the U.S. border. One journalist reporting on the crusade's impact called Luis "the Billy Graham of Latin America." Others picked up the story, and the word spread. Slowly, the Palau team's dream of crusade evangelism was becoming a reality. Years of hard work and perseverance were beginning to pay off. They could reach the masses with the Good News about Jesus Christ.

Early in 1971, Luis returned for a two week crusade in Lima, Peru. The large bullring held more than 103,000 people. And nearly 5,000 people made public decisions for Jesus Christ.

Suddenly, the news media in Latin America grew interested in the Palau team. Forty-two newsmen gathered for a press conference about the crusade. It was unheard of for such a group to cover an evangelistic meeting.

Christians in Peru had been ridiculed or ignored

FORTY-TWO NEWSMEN GATHERED FOR A PRESS CONFERENCE
ABOUT THE CRUSADE.

by the media. Now the Palau team received nation-wide coverage. Parts of Luis' messages were broadcast on fifty-five radio stations. As Billy Graham had done in the United States, the Palau team began to do overseas—use interviews with the media to spread the Good News about Jesus Christ.

Two years later, a twelve-day crusade was scheduled in Santo Domingo in the Dominican Republic. The Palau team invited key people in the city, including the president, to a breakfast before the crusade. The president didn't attend, but sent a lawyer as his representative. After the breakfast, Luis spoke to the president's lawyer.

"The president would like to meet with you before you leave the country," she said. "But he can see you only on Sunday, immediately after mass, in the chapel of the presidential palace. If you come to mass with him, he will have forty-five minutes to talk with you. His chauffeur will pick you up at 8:30 Sunday morning."

THE PALAU TEAM BEGAN TO USE INTERVIEWS TO SPREAD THE GOOD NEWS ABOUT JESUS CHRIST.

"I'll be there!" Luis said. To Luis' knowledge, no one had ever witnessed to this man before. What an exciting opportunity for the Gospel in the Dominican Republic!

After the initial excitement wore off, Luis began to worry. *Some non-Catholic Christians might hear about me sitting through mass and become upset with me. I can't go through with this.* When Luis talked with some of the pastors in Santo Domingo, they confirmed his fear about the meeting. They told him not to go.

Later, Luis consulted with a Christian lawyer who worked closely with the government. This man advised him, "You should go to mass and witness to the president." Palau knew what the Lord wanted him to do, but he turned coward. When the chauffeur arrived on Sunday morning, Luis sent him away.

Discouragement swept over him like a flood. His joy in the Lord disappeared. That afternoon

DISCOURAGEMENT SWEPT OVER HIM LIKE A FLOOD.

Luis prayed, "Lord, forgive me. I'll never turn down an opportunity to witness to somebody because I fear what others might think."

A few years later, while visiting another South American country, Luis spoke privately with the president, a military man. "Mr. President," Luis asked, "do you know Jesus Christ?"

The president smiled and said, "Palau, I've led such a hard life; I don't think God wants to know me very much."

"Mr. President, no matter what you've done, Christ died on the cross to receive the punishment that should be ours for the wrong we have done." Luis said, "Sir, would you like to receive Christ now?"

The president paused and quite seriously said, "If Christ will receive me, I want to become a real Christian."

Right then, the pair of men bowed their heads and prayed together. This general opened his heart

"IF CHRIST WILL RECEIVE ME,
I WANT TO BECOME A REAL CHRISTIAN."

to the Son of God and received Christ into his life.

The president had believed that God would never receive him because of his past. But when he and Luis finished praying, he stood up and in the custom of his country gave Luis a tremendous hug. "Thank you," he said. "Now I know that Christ has really received me and forgiven me."

In the months that followed, Luis spoke at other large crusades in Nicaragua, Guatemala, Chile, and Peru. Thousands of people heard the Gospel and accepted Jesus Christ. Then in 1975, Luis took a break from his Latin America work, and preached the Good News in thirteen cities in four nations of the United Kingdom during a two week period. Luis became convinced that God was calling him to evangelize the British Isles as well as Latin America.

About this time, *Time* magazine reported that Latin America was turning to Christ with one exception: the country of Uruguay. Fully thirty percent

LUIS PREACHED THE GOOD NEWS IN THIRTEEN CITIES IN FOUR NATIONS OF THE UNITED KINGDOM.

of its people claimed to be atheists—a figure that was unheard of outside the communist world. Luis determined to proclaim the Gospel in this country.

Flying from city to city in Uruguay was impossible, so Luis and his team traveled in an assortment of older vehicles over sixteen hundred miles of roads to present the Gospel to more than one hundred thousand men, women, and young people. The six back-to-back crusades were exhausting, but the team was encouraged at the response to the Gospel.

After preaching throughout Uruguay, Luis returned to OC International board meetings in California. He had accepted the presidency with the condition that it would be reviewed in two years. After prayerful consideration, Luis asked the board to release him from his OC leadership responsibilities. He found it impossible to manage his thirty-member evangelistic team and also lead the mission.

Everyone on the board agreed that it would be

LUIS WAS DETERMINED TO PROCLAIM THE GOSPEL.

best if the Luis Palau Evangelistic Association (LPEA) became a separate missions organization. Effective October 1, 1978, the organization was started, and Luis Palau began a new ministry with headquarters in Portland, Oregon, where he and Pat had first met and married.

A couple of weeks after LPEA became a separate organization, Luis and the team returned to Bolivia for three weeks of meetings. Although some amazing results happened four years earlier, nothing could have prepared them for the national revival in October 1978.

In La Paz, the capital city, police had to close the stadium gates each night. They turned hundreds of people away from the public crusade meetings. On Saturday and Sunday, two services were held each afternoon and evening. The lines of people stretched for blocks to enter the stadium.

In Santa Cruz and Cochabamba, Bolivia, an overwhelming response also happened. During the

THE LINES OF PEOPLE STRETCHED FOR BLOCKS
TO ENTER THE STADIUM.

crusade, they broke nearly every previous Luis Palau crusade record—for attendance (180,000), decisions for Christ (18,916), and the ratio of decisions to attendance (10.5 percent).

Throughout Bolivia, many stories were told about changed lives as people received Christ. But two decisions were unforgettable for Luis and probably weren't in the crusade statistics.

At a mid-morning press conference in a prestigious downtown La Paz hotel, journalists' pens were scratching the news. Luis began answering questions—sometimes barbed—from some of Bolivia's leading editors and writers. A little girl slipped into the room. Luis recognized her as the daughter of the hotel elevator operator and thought, *What could she possibly want?*

He picked up a copy of one of his books and autographed it, then handed it to the girl and whispered, "The Lord bless you, sweetheart." He smiled at the girl, but she held her ground. She

LUIS BEGAN ANSWERING QUESTIONS FROM BOLIVIA'S LEADING EDITORS AND WRITERS.

didn't want a book and a smile.

"Mr. Palau, what I really wanted to ask you was how I could receive Jesus in my heart." The previous evening, the girl, who looked less than eleven years old, had watched Palau counsel people on national television. He spoke to a high school student and led him to Christ. Now she too wanted to receive the Savior.

Instantly the plans for the press conference evaporated. Quickly, Luis asked the media to leave the room. Publicity was important to the crusade, but Palau knew the reporters could ask their questions another day. As 2 Corinthians 6:2 says, "Now is the day of salvation."

While in Bolivia, the team held another President's Prayer Breakfast with Bolivia's new president, General Juan Pereda Asbun, twenty-five high-ranking military officers, eight cabinet members, and many other leaders.

During a twenty-minute address, Palau read

SHE WANTED TO RECEIVE THE SAVIOR.

Deuteronomy 28:1-14, then outlined the national benefits when a country obeys the Lord. In response, President Pereda stood up and reaffirmed the importance of setting "personal and national spiritual priorities." Then the president publicly endorsed the crusades.

Afterward, in a private meeting, Luis asked the president about his own relationship with Jesus Christ, then explained the Good News of forgiveness through the blood of Jesus Christ. There in his presidential office, President Pereda bowed his head and gave his life to Christ. The social position of a person didn't matter to Luis. For him, there was no greater thrill than to lead someone to Christ.

A few weeks later, thousands more trusted Christ in Acapulco and Veracruz, Mexico. Luis felt God's call on his life and the Lord's blessing on his team.

THOUSANDS MORE TRUSTED CHRIST IN ACAPULCO
AND VERACRUZ, MEXICO.

CHURCHES WERE CLOSING BY THE HUNDREDS.

8

As the 1970s drew to a close, Palau and his team held meetings in Caracas, Venezuela, as well as fifteen youth rallies in ten cities of England during two weeks. More than 2,700 people registered their commitment to Jesus Christ. Many leading evangelicals in Britain talked with Luis about the dismal trend of the church in Great Britain. Churches were closing by the hundreds, and often church furnishings were shipped to America, Japan, and Western

Europe to be sold as antiques.

Luis thought, *If it takes a third-generation transplanted European who was born in the Third World and who now claims American citizenship to help turn the tide in Britain, so be it.* The next spring, Palau and his team returned to England for another series of crusades in Scotland. In a week and a half, nearly two thousand people committed their lives to Christ.

Behind closed doors, a dozen Scottish ministers met with Luis. They voiced their opposition to his organized mass evangelism. As they talked, Luis was surprised by the differences they had over basic questions. At least half of the ministers honestly told Luis that they didn't accept the Bible as the trustworthy Word of God. Was it any surprise that churches throughout this region were failing? Thousands of people's lives were transformed through the Gospel message from the Palau team.

Later that year, Luis traveled to Guayaquil,

PALAU AND HIS TEAM RETURNED TO ENGLAND
FOR ANOTHER SERIES OF CRUSADES IN SCOTLAND.

Ecuador, for a crusade. After the evening meetings, the live call-in counseling program was broadcast for twelve consecutive nights over twenty-five repeater stations to all of Ecuador and much of neighboring Colombia and Peru. More than 2,800 made decisions for Christ at the Guayaquil crusade, and only heaven will know the results from the call-in counseling. When the nightly broadcasts stopped, 180 people called in to complain. They didn't want the program to end. This type of response was unheard of for almost any other kind of programming!

Back in the U.S., Pat Palau was fighting the battle of her life against breast cancer, so Luis cut back on his travel schedule. Luis began to think, *With Pat so sick, why not make more extensive use of the media this next year?* That would give him more time to be available to his wife. His team members agreed.

Besides Pat's ongoing cancer treatments, there

PAT PALAU WAS FIGHTING FOR HER LIFE AGAINST CANCER.

were other reasons for Luis to curtail his crusade schedule. Pat told Luis, "If you don't stay at home, these boys will go straight to the world." He panicked to think of his sons walking away from the Lord. He spent some time at home in Portland, Oregon.

Together Pat and Luis decided to watch Kevin and Keith for the next six months. If they saw no change, Luis would drop all of his crusade commitments. It was a desperate decision, but they didn't see any other option.

Soon after that, Christian musician Keith Green came to Portland. Keith and Kevin attended his concert and a retreat. They were both deeply moved and dedicated their lives to God. Shortly after this experience, they applied to Wheaton College, a leading Christian school. Luis and Pat breathed a sigh of relief. But the struggles continued.

Because of Pat's ongoing battle with cancer, Luis cut back his 1981 crusade schedule to two

KEVIN AND KEITH DEDICATED THEIR LIVES TO GOD.

crusades. He traveled to Glasgow, Scotland, for five weeks as a part of the LPEA three-year strategy to re-evangelize Scotland. During the thirty-six day crusade, more than 5,325 people committed their lives to Jesus Christ. Evangelism was back on the map in Scotland.

After the Scotland crusade, Luis thought about evangelism in America. Ever since he had first felt God's call to crusade evangelism, Palau had poured himself into overseas evangelism. He planned to stay out of the States until Billy Graham slowed down. That was twenty years ago and Billy Graham was still going as strong as ever. Luis wondered when he would get a chance. *Was my dream of evangelizing America's cities always going to be only a dream?* he wondered.

With some hesitation, he accepted an invitation to San Diego for LPEA's first full-scale American crusade. More than twelve hundred people committed their lives to Christ during the crusade, but Luis

"WAS MY DREAM OF EVANGELIZING AMERICA'S CITIES ALWAYS GOING TO BE ONLY A DREAM?"

felt that somehow he had disobeyed the Lord. Yes, the Lord was opening the door of opportunity for ministry in the United States, but it would be on God's schedule—not Luis'.

That fall, Kevin and Keith flew out of the nest for their first semester at Wheaton College, near Chicago. A few days after they returned home for the holidays, a bone scan revealed Pat had no signs of cancer. The Palau family celebrated Christmas and New Year's in a big way that year.

The next year, Luis started with a new level of intensity. Seven crusades were scheduled on four continents. He made trips to the countries of Australia, Finland, Paraguay, England, and Guatemala, and to the states of Washington and Wisconsin.

The series of crusades in Guatemala City was held in conjunction with the hundred-year celebration of the Good News coming to the nation. A few months earlier, the LPEA team had wondered if the celebration would be canceled because of political

THE PALAU FAMILY CELEBRATED CHRISTMAS
AND THE NEW YEAR IN A BIG WAY.

violence. But after months of upheaval, finally Guatemala was enjoying a period of relative peace. The Central American field director, Benjamin Orozco, assured Luis that the crusade could proceed as planned without incident.

The week-long crusade received more media attention than any of the previous 175 crusades and rallies. Each night, fifteen radio stations broadcast the messages live from the crusade. More than twenty evangelistic messages that Luis had taped aired on two television stations.

Early one Sunday, hundreds of Christians prepared to celebrate one hundred years of the Gospel in their country. Before this celebration, no one knew how many committed Christians were in Guatemala. For years, Luis had been saying that it would be the first nation to achieve fifty-one percent of born-again Christians. But nothing could have prepared Luis for what he and his team saw that morning.

THE WEEK-LONG CRUSADE RECEIVED MORE MEDIA ATTENTION THAN ANY OF THE PREVIOUS 175 CRUSADES.

Tens of thousands, then hundreds of thousands of people started to fill the park. Military helicopters flew overhead, trying to get some estimate of the crowd size—first 500,000, then 600,000, finally 700,000 people! After the event, historian Virgil Zapara called it the largest gathering of born-again Christians in the history not only of Guatemala, but of all Latin America. The largest gathering of the church in Guatemala reaffirmed Luis' belief in mass evangelism and its effectiveness.

His call to evangelistic work was clear from the Scriptures, church history, and experience, but it was not without critics. Some people have severely criticized Luis Palau and others for meeting with presidents, prime ministers, and other top government officials. Luis clearly believes that everyone needs the healing power and freedom of a personal relationship with Jesus Christ—including the leaders of nations.

Over the next several years, Luis and his team

MILITARY HELICOPTERS FLEW OVERHEAD,
TRYING TO GET SOME ESTIMATE OF THE CROWD SIZE.

continued to focus on ministry overseas. They had three crusades in America during three years and planned to have five more over the next five years. But the green light was flashing in other countries.

In the fall of 1983, the Palau Association blanketed London with nine regional crusades and an ambitious seven-week crusade six months later. At the *Mission to London,* Luis preached every night for six weeks in Queen's Park Ranger's Stadium. People from every creed, color, religious background, and walk of life trusted Jesus Christ—a top rock star, a famous actress, a disillusioned policeman, a car dealer, a truck driver, and a bus driver were interviewed on the same night by the BBC.

The official crusade photographer, an Australian soccer player, a young businesswoman, a gentleman whose wife had prayed for his salvation for twenty-one years, twenty-five boys at a British boarding school, a young gang member who had helped disrupt the meeting earlier that same

PEOPLE FROM EVERY CREED, COLOR, AND RELIGIOUS BACKGROUND TRUSTED JESUS CHRIST.

evening, a runaway teenager, and more than a few religious ministers also made decisions for Jesus Christ.

By the final night, the cumulative attendance for the *Mission to London* had topped 518,000, and more than 28,000 people had made public commitments to Jesus Christ. The last week of June, Luis' messages were broadcast to the entire British Commonwealth—fifty nations.

Beyond this huge effort to bring the Gospel to the British Commonwealth, the Palau team also had similar missions to Latin America in 1985 and Asia in 1986. They saw tremendous results.

Sometimes the Palau team is accused of talking too much about numbers. In many parts of the world, people are being born by the thousands and dying by the thousands. But as Luis says, they are being won to Jesus Christ by ones and twos. As the Palau team reaches the masses, they want to give exclusive glory to God for his moving in

LUIS' MESSAGES WERE BROADCAST TO THE ENTIRE
BRITISH COMMONWEALTH—FIFTY NATIONS.

the hearts of men and women through the presentation of the Good News about Jesus Christ.

During 1985, Vice President George Bush and Luis spoke to students at Wheaton College. Both men received honorary doctorates during the commencement exercises. For Luis, the degree marked his second honorary doctorate. He received the first one from Talbot Theological Seminary in 1977. At the Wheaton ceremony, Luis found it a special moment because that day his twin sons, Keith and Kevin, graduated with honors.

Over the next months, Luis and his team saw amazing results for the Gospel during crusades in Switzerland and Argentina. Returning home, he poured himself into his final preparations for the first Asian crusade in Singapore.

As Luis preached in the National Stadium of Singapore, his messages were broadcast through a cooperative effort with Far East Broadcasting Company, Trans World Radio, HCJB, and other

DURING 1985, VICE PRESIDENT BUSH AND LUIS SPOKE TO STUDENTS AT WHEATON COLLEGE.

missionary radio and television ministries. The meetings were simultaneously translated into eight major Asian languages and broadcast throughout Asia.

During the meetings, 11,902 people publicly gave their lives to Jesus Christ. After the meetings, Luis and the team received invitations for other crusades in Hong Kong, India, Indonesia, Japan, the Philippines, Thailand, and other Asian nations. An opportunity for ministry was opening to Luis and the team in a different part of the world.

Early the next year, Luis went to Fiji and New Zealand in the South Pacific to conduct four weeks of crusades. These were hard days of intense meetings for Luis. Four to six daily events drained his energy, and his voice was practically gone. There wasn't a single day's break in four weeks. During these days of ministry, 11,426 people committed their lives to Jesus Christ. With results like that, Luis found his energy renewed for mass evangelism.

DURING THE MEETINGS, 11,902 PEOPLE PUBLICLY GAVE THEIR LIVES TO JESUS.

Also that spring, Luis preached the Good News for the first time in Africa. He went to Nairobi, Kenya, and preached at a one-night evangelistic rally. Three hundred and fifty people accepted the Lord.

During this time, Luis received the first of many invitations to preach the Gospel in Eastern Europe. As the Iron Curtain fell, Luis and his team found many people hungry for the Good News of salvation through Christ. Little did he know that during the next four years, he would personally see more than 101,000 Eastern Europeans commit their lives to Jesus Christ. The doors of ministry were opening wider and wider for Luis Palau.

IN KENYA, 350 PEOPLE ACCEPTED THE LORD.

LUIS CONTINUED TO TURN HIS HEART
AND THOUGHTS TOWARD HOME.

9

As Luis and his team geared up to finish the 1980s with a flurry of crusades, Luis continued to turn his heart and thoughts toward home. He had studied the rise and fall of Christianity in Western Civilization. He saw that America was in between the mid-century revival of Christianity and total secularism.

While preaching in other nations, Luis felt that he could no longer ignore crusade invitations in the

United States. His team must go to the nations of the world but also to America—not immediately, but in an organized, planned strategy under the guidance of the Spirit of the Lord.

Luis' burden for America increased as he and the team had another crusade in Guatemala. Nearly 250,000 people packed Mateo Flores Stadium to hear the Gospel. Even more people crowded on a nearby hillside. More than 6,600 people made a public commitment to Jesus Christ and another 1,600 did the same at pre-crusade events.

Despite his growing concern for America, Luis didn't want to move ahead without talking to Billy Graham. For some reason he felt nervous about calling the older evangelist.

Much to Luis' surprise, a couple weeks later, Billy Graham called him in Los Angeles. Luis still doesn't know how Billy Graham got the phone number.

"Luis," he said, "I just saw that article in

PEOPLE CROWDED ON A NEARBY HILLSIDE.

Christianity Today." The article spoke about the recent Palau team crusades. They had just returned from Poland and Hungary, and they had accepted invitations to preach the Gospel in the first public stadium evangelistic crusades in the history of the Soviet Union.

"Goodness gracious," Billy exclaimed. "You're all over the world these days."

Luis took a deep breath and then began. "Billy, I've got to ask your blessing on something." Then Luis explained his long-standing burden for America. "I feel the time has come that I should accept more crusade invitations in the States and really go for the bigger cities. But I want to feel that I have your full blessing."

Billy said, "Well, you don't need it. But if you want it, you've got it. Get on with it! Everybody talks about evangelizing America. Now let's really do it."

Luis knew Billy was right. If Palau had to

THEY HAD JUST RETURNED FROM POLAND AND HUNGARY.

describe the situation in America with one word, it would be *confusion*. According to Gallup Polls, nine out of ten Americans believed in God. Eight out of ten called themselves Christians. Four out of ten claimed they went to church on any given Sunday. But Luis wondered, *Where is the reality? Where is the witness to a watching world?*

That April, the LPEA board of directors mandated that the Palau evangelistic association begin accepting invitations for as many as four American metropolitan area crusades a year. Ironically, Palau and his team received this mandate with the knowledge of commitments for crusades in many other places in the world.

In the middle of August, Luis and several team members said an earnest prayer for safety before flying to Bogotá, Colombia. In a 48-hour period, a number of political assassinations had taken place, including the killing of the leading presidential candidate.

LUIS AND TEAM MEMBERS SAID AN EARNEST PRAYER
BEFORE LEAVING FOR BOGOTÁ, COLOMBIA.

The drug cartel had declared an all-out war. In the middle of one of Colombia's worst crises, Palau preached the Good News about Jesus Christ to capacity crowds. The team saw an incredible 10,288 people dedicate their lives to the Lord that week.

A few weeks later, Luis and his team arrived in the Soviet Union for a historic series of meetings in four republics. They received a telegram from Billy Graham that said, "We are praying that God will abundantly bless you and that many people will find Christ. We are praying that your meetings will open doors for others that may come later." Luis felt thankful for the wonderful friend that Billy Graham had become to him.

That Christmas marked the first time that the Palau family wasn't together since the twins had been born. The third Palau son, Andrew, had graduated from the University of Oregon and moved to Boston to "seek his fortune." Pat and Luis had

LUIS AND HIS TEAM ARRIVED IN THE SOVIET UNION.

unvoiced concerns about whether Andrew intended to walk with the Lord, but there was little they could do. They committed Andrew to the Lord, kept the lines of communication open, loved him, and continued praying.

During the first part of 1992, Luis and the team continued a fast-paced tour throughout the United Kingdom. As his theme, Luis talked about the need of today's church—the mighty fire of the Holy Spirit. Palau said, "As Christians, the Holy Spirit's fire is in us. We must not let that fire die down!" Instead, he encouraged the believers to "fan into flame the gift of God, which is in you" (2 Timothy 1:6).

Throughout the years, Luis has spoken to many different gatherings such as Urbana and National Prayer Breakfasts, and conventions of the National Religious Broadcasters and the Evangelical Press Association. But in the summer of 1992, Luis was one of the speakers at the first Promise Keepers

LUIS ENCOURAGED THE BELIEVERS TO FAN INTO FLAME
THE GIFT OF GOD WHICH IS IN THEM.

conference in Boulder, Colorado. As he saw tens of thousands of Christian men commit themselves to be godly men of integrity, it gave him hope for America's spiritual revival. He thought, *God is about to do something great through this movement in our land!*

On the border of the United States, the Palau team held a crusade in Reynosa, Mexico. Mayor Ramon Perez Garcia welcomed the team to his city of 750,000 people. On the opening night of the crusade, Mayor Perez named Luis a guest of honor before a near capacity crowd of 14,000 people. "What energy we have here!" he said to Luis.

"It's the energy of God," Palau responded.

"Yes, yes," the mayor replied. That evening, his wife came forward to receive Christ.

On the other side of the Rio Grande in McAllen, Texas, area churches united for a series of meetings with Luis Palau. The four rallies in Memorial Stadium were attended by 32,500 people. The live

"IT'S THE ENERGY OF GOD," LUIS RESPONDED.

call-in counseling program called *Night Talk* pre-empted *The Tonight Show* with Jay Leno on the NBC affiliate. Nine people prayed with Luis on the air to receive Jesus Christ as their Savior. In the studio, two cameramen and a control room operator also trusted in Christ.

In ten days in the Rio Grande Valley, more than 5,400 people made a public declaration of their lives to Christ. That fall, thousands more were brought into God's kingdom during crusades in Panama, Portugal, and Phoenix.

At the Phoenix crusade press conference in the America West Arena, Jerry Colangelo, the owner of the NBA Phoenix Suns, introduced Luis Palau. Luis spoke of his desire to bring America back to her days of glory. "A spirit of despondency seems to permeate this nation," he explained. "Our currency says, 'In God We Trust,' but we have gotten away from trusting God. Americans have lost hope."

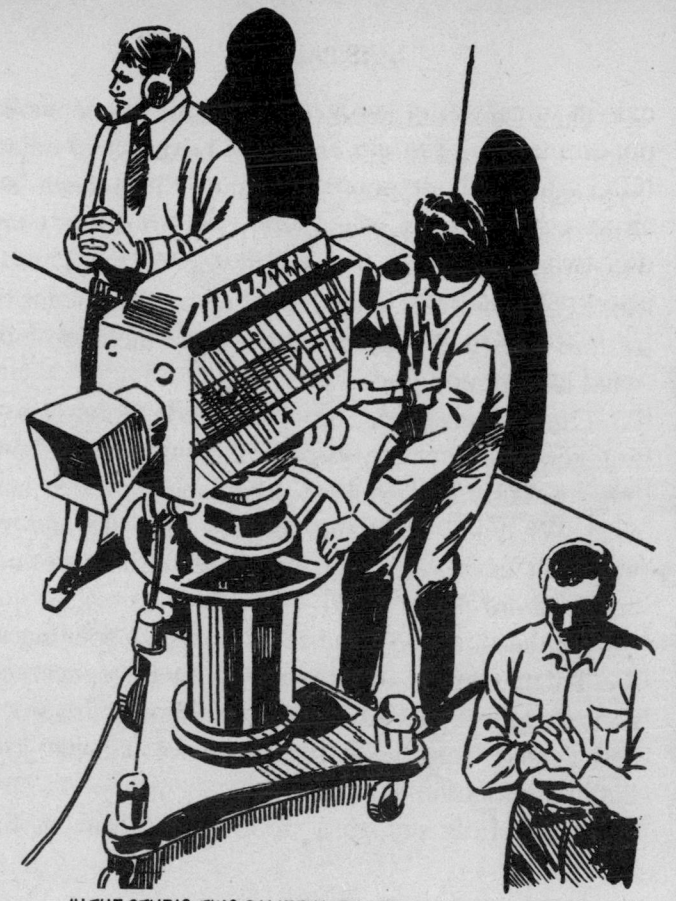

IN THE STUDIO, TWO CAMERAMEN AND A CONTROL OPERATOR TRUSTED IN CHRIST.

Then Luis continued on the theme of reconciliation. "We need to get over this business of being hyphenated Americans," he said. "I've been an American for thirty years. My passport doesn't say Hispanic-American. It says citizen of the United States of America." Then he called on Americans to restore a spirit of holiness and restore their sense of what is right and good.

Finally Luis said, "America needs Good News, not good advice. My dream is that people from other nations will look at a revived America and ask, 'What is happening there?' And the answer they will hear: 'A nation has been turned around, and God did it.'"

As the doors to America continued opening to the Palau team, Luis continued to be concerned about his third son, Andrew. Pat said of their son, "I had a sense from the Lord that he was a sweet guy but had not come to Christ."

When Luis prepared in 1993 to speak at the

"A NATION HAS BEEN TURNED AROUND, AND GOD DID IT."

Jamaica crusade, the Palaus invited Andrew to take a vacation from his job in Boston. They knew Andrew loved to fish, and he agreed to come to Jamaica.

During fifteen days in eleven cities, more than 245,000 people attended the meetings. Andrew came to every single meeting. One night, Andrew walked forward with the people to recommit his life to Jesus Christ.

Besides deep sea fishing, Andrew discovered something else in Jamaica—a lovely girl named Wendy. A few months after the crusade, Wendy invited Andrew to a Christian retreat. During this retreat, Andrew poured out his past to the Lord and received forgiveness. In 1994, Andrew and Wendy were married. Andrew has been working part-time with LPEA and attending graduate school at Multnomah. He worked with LPEA on the preparations for the eight-week *Say Yes Crusade* in Chicago in April and May of 1996.

THE PALAUS KNEW ANDREW LOVED TO FISH AND INVITED HIM
FOR A VACATION IN JAMAICA.

Luis said, "To me, Andrew's conversion is a beautiful picture of what I'd like to see God to do for the people of America, young and old. There are thousands of other Andrews who need Jesus Christ. My heart goes out to them—and to their families."

Through more than thirty years of mass evangelism, Luis Palau has personally addressed more than twelve million people. More than 700,000 people have made known decisions for Jesus Christ during some 360 crusades and rallies. He has an estimated daily radio audience of twenty-two million people. In addition, he's testing a national weekly evangelistic television outreach that could reach millions more with the Gospel.

Luis says, "With all my heart, I'm convinced the resurrected Lord Jesus Christ has the power to effect massive positive changes in America." The years ahead will show what further part Luis Palau will have in bringing that message to America and the rest of the world.

"I'M CONVINCED THE RESURRECTED LORD JESUS CHRIST HAS THE POWER TO EFFECT MASSIVE POSITIVE CHANGES IN AMERICA."

AWESOME BOOKS FOR KIDS!

The Young Reader's Christian Library
Action, Adventure, and Fun Reading!

This series for young readers ages 8 to 12 is action-packed, fast-paced, and Christ-centered! With exciting illustrations on every other page following the text, kids won't be able to put these books down! Over 100 illustrations per book. All books are paperbound. The unique size (4 ³¹⁄₁₆" x 5 ³¹⁄₄₈") makes these books easy to take anywhere!

A Great Selection to Satisfy All Kids!

Abraham Lincoln	*Heidi*	*Pollyanna*
Ben-Hur	*Hudson Taylor*	*Prudence of Plymouth*
Billy Graham	*In His Steps*	*Plantation*
Billy Sunday	*Jesus*	*Robinson Crusoe*
Christopher Columbus	*Joseph*	*Roger Williams*
Corrie ten Boom	*Lydia*	*Ruth*
David Brainerd	*Miriam*	*Samuel Morris*
David Livingstone	*Moses*	*The Swiss Family*
Deborah	*Paul*	*Robinson*
Elijah	*Peter*	*Taming the Land*
Esther	*The Pilgrim's Progress*	*Thunder in the Valley*
Florence Nightingale	*Pocahontas*	*Wagons West*